WARNING:

This book has not been approved by the

Department of Homeland Security. You are

reading at your own risk.

ANOTHER WARNING:

To avoid having the FBI open a file in your name, you might wanna put away that credit card and use cash to buy this one.

Mickey Z

Stephen Jay Gould sez: "I am somehow less interested in the weight and convolutions of Einstein's brain than in the near certainty that people of equal talent have lived and died in cotton fields and sweatshops."

Charles Bukowski sez: "Almost everybody is born a genius and buried an idiot."

No Innocent Bystanders

Riding Shotgun in the Land of Denial

Mickey Z

This one's for The Expendables

Other books by Mickey Z.

Fiction

CPR for Dummies (Raw Dog Screaming Press, 2008)

Non-fiction

50 American Revolutions You're Not Supposed to Know: Reclaiming American Patriotism (Disinformation Books, 2005)

The Seven Deadly Spins: Exposing the Lies Behind War Propaganda (Common Courage Press, 2004)

A Gigantic Mistake: Articles & Essays for Your Intellectual Self-Defense (Library Empyreal, 2004)

The Murdering of My Years: Artists & Activists Making Ends Meet (Soft Skull Press, 2003)

Saving Private Power: The Hidden History of "The Good War" (Soft Skull Press, 2000)

His work has appeared in the following anthologies:

What Would Bill Hicks Say? (Soft Skull Press, 2006)

Tutto in Vendita (Nuovi Mondi Media, 2005)

Underground (Disinformation Books, 2005)

Under the Influence (Disinformation Books, 2004)

The Book of Lists (Disinformation Books, 2003)

Abuse Your Illusions (Disinformation Books, 2003)

Everything You Know is Wrong (Disinformation Books, 2002)

You Are Being Lied To (Disinformation Books, 2001)

No Innocent Bystanders

Riding Shotgun

in the Land of Denial

by Mickey Z.

FIRST EDITION

Published by CWG Press, 1204 NE 11th Ave #2, Fort Lauderdale, FL 33304

978-0-9788186-2-3

5 4 3 2 1

Acknowledgments

My deep appreciation to Chuck Gregory for making this book happen, to my ever-supportive Dad, to Michele, my wife and partner, and to the enduring memory and influence of my Mom.

TABLE OF CONTENTS

Author's Preface: Hard Rain

On the liner notes for *The Freewheelin' Bob Dylan* album, it's explained that the song "A Hard Rain's A-Gonna Fall" was written during the 1962 Cuban Missile Crisis. "A desperate kind of song," Dylan called it.

"Every line in it is actually the start of a whole song," he explained. "But when I wrote it, I thought I wouldn't have enough time alive to write all those songs so I put all I could into this one."

This book has been created in that spirit…and is thusly filled with the kind of material guaranteed to help me maintain my status as a virtually anonymous figure across the globe.

Picking Out the Hayseeds

In 1853, the future founders of the Brooklyn Botanic
Garden set free several pairs of the previously unknown
European house sparrow *(Passer domesticus)* inside
Brooklyn's Greenwood Cemetery. By picking the hayseeds
out of horse droppings, the tiny birds thrived and are now
one of the nation's most ubiquitous creatures.

Extinction is forever

Estimates vary, but roughly 50,000 animal and plant species become extinct each year. That's over 130 per day, about 6 per hour.

Here's a fun game to improve your math and reading skills (both come in handy when taking tests like the SATs): Time yourself as you read this book and calculate how many species that were still around when you began reading have since become history. For added enjoyment, read quickly so less species are gone by the last page.

Fear of a Keith Moon Planet

Let's say we're back in the 1970s, and you've got dreams of being in a rock band. Besides possessing at least a modicum of musical ability, there are several other prerequisites to fulfill, e.g. long hair, sex, heavy drinking, sex, drug use, sex, intolerable drum solos, sex, and, of course, an innate ability to utterly demolish hotel rooms without an ounce of guilt or remorse.

How many yarns have been spun and books written and documentaries shot about classic rockers like Led Zeppelin turning their rented rooms into potential Superfund sites? The legend of The Who's Keith Moon's was built as much on his motel madness as his drumming dexterity. As TheWho.net explains, Moon was known for "stripping naked in airports and on television shows, destroying hotel rooms, swinging from chandeliers, throwing televisions out of hotel windows, (and) putting cherry bombs in toilets" while ClassicRockPage.com estimates that the total damage "wreaked by Moon around the world over a span of 14 years was … about $500,000."

Did George Bernard Shaw know something we didn't when he declared: "I don't know if there are men on the moon, but if there are, they must using the earth as their lunatic asylum"? Consider this recent come-on from a British travel website: "Los Angeles has more rock 'n' roll landmarks—and more trashed hotel rooms—than any other city, making it a mecca (*sic*) for music fans and trivia buffs." Thanks to folks like Tommy Lee and Sid Vicious, it's become socially acceptable—admirable even—to leave your borrowed digs in far worse shape than when you found them. But it's all harmless fun, right? Besides, who cares about a hotel room once you're gone? Hmm … I smell a metaphor brewing.

But first, I suggest you look at your watch, check the time, and consider this: Since yesterday at this hour, 13 million tons of toxic chemicals were released across the globe; two hundred thousand acres of rainforest were destroyed; more than 100 plant or animal species went extinct; and 45,000 human beings died of starvation (most of them, by the way, were children).

We now return to our regularly scheduled metaphor (or is this an allegory?):

Imagine Planet Earth as an enormous, overbooked, and understaffed Holiday Inn Express. Now imagine the mass of humanity as, say, a younger Ozzy Osbourne on tour... without his wife around to supervise. Go one step further and picture the politicians, generals, CEOs, and all those other "deciders" who are unable to see beyond the next fiscal quarter as none other than Keith Moon the Loon himself. Indeed, Hotel Gaia is in for a long, long night.

At some point, however, the hotel bill will come due. And make no mistake about it—based even on the tiny sampling of damage detailed above—this metaphorical debt will give new meaning to the phrase "dark side of the Moon." Are you ready?

Wish you were here

- Sea Mink
- Rodrigues Pigeon
- Rodrigues Little Owl
- Rodrigues Parrot
- Panay Giant Fruit Bat,
- Poko Noctuid Moth
- Procellaris Grotis Noctuid Moth
- Great Auk
- Bubal Hartebeest
- Mauritius Blue Pigeon
- Mauritian Shelduck
- Egyptian Barbary Sheep
- Amesterdam Island Duck
- Mauritian Duck
- Cuban Red Macaw
- Ascension Flightless Crake
- Eastern Bettong
- Réunion Flightless Ibis
- Desert Rat-kangaroo
- Eastern Elk

My first anti-war protest

By the time I was 9...I understood these 2 things:

1. The war in Vietnam was not popular

2. Being on TV is a big deal to most people

Hanging with my friends on Crescent Street—just 2 blocks from the 59th Street Bridge connecting Queens to the East Side of Manhattan—I hatched a cynical scheme to capitalize on the above two facts.

About 6 of us staged an anti-war protest amidst the high volume of motor vehicles streaming down Crescent Street on their way to the city (Queens is one of NYC's five boroughs but for us, only Manhattan is "the city").

We made signs and posters and held them up to passing cars and trucks as we yelled "End the war" in our pre-pubescent voices.

"Someone will call the news," I promised, "and we'll be on TV tonight."

One of my fellow radicals wasn't a regular on the block...a little older than me. I can't remember his name but I can still see his face when I scolded him for writing:

SPOT THE WAR!

Our children's crusade lasted about 30 minutes and neither ended the war or landed us on TV...but we had a blast.

Lesson: Protesting can be a bonding experience but it rarely achieves its intended goal.

Top Ten Ways to Change the World

1. Wear a "Free Tibet" t-shirt

2. Switch to recycled toilet paper

3. Watch Jon Stewart and Stephen Colbert

4. Adopt a Third World orphan

5. Start a discussion about Africa

6. Eat free range chicken

7. Drive a hybrid SUV

8. Subscribe to *The Nation*

9. Chant for peace in your yoga class

10. Vote Democrat

Big Daddy

Once upon a time...

"But we're hungry, Big Daddy" the children cried, their emaciated bodies a testament to their neglect.

"We all have to make sacrifices," Big Daddy declared, "and if I spend money on food for you, I'll be too broke to join the gym. And if Big Daddy's muscles don't stay strong, you kids will have a lot more to worry about than being a little hungry."

"We're not a little hungry, Big Daddy. We're starving. We're dying."

Big Daddy eyed this particularly brazen child before bashing him with a clenched right fist. The child sailed across the room and landed in a bloody heap against the wall.

"I didn't want to do that, children," announced Big Daddy as he flexed his triceps in the mirror. "But if you allow one bad apple to act as a cancer, the whole barrel will rot. Sometimes it's necessary to exert force to promote peace and stabilize a situation."

"Oh, Big Daddy, we're just asking for you to fix the hole in the roof so we don't freeze again tonight."

"What? Exert myself in such a petty affair? What if Big Daddy hurt himself? Who would fight off our neighbors? What would you kids do then?"

"But I like our neighbors. They don't want to hurt us."

Big Daddy hit this child with his left hand. "Don't ever let me hear you say that. You kids aren't smart enough to know danger when you see it and if that sneaky neighbor ever heard you speak kindly of him, he'd take advantage of our weakness. We must stick together to fight the evil he's building next door. If even one family member isn't behind me, I can't use these muscles. I need all of you to support me. Do you understand?"

Big Daddy's bellowing scared the children and they agreed. He told them some of the stories that his parents had told him and the children saw that it was long family tradition for the Big Daddy to spend all his time, energy, and money to build himself up in order to protect his weaker family members. It truly is sometimes necessary to destroy something in order to save it. The children began to see what "family values" really means.

The two kids who were hit crawled back and apologized to Big Daddy for forcing him to hurt them. Another child tried to thank Big Daddy for keeping his biceps so strong, but the words wouldn't come out. The child was too sick and too cold. Big Daddy hinted that this particular child wasn't fit to be in their family. And, as Big Daddy conveniently turned the other way to flex his back muscles, the fit children ganged up and beat their unfit sibling before sending him from their home.

"Go out there," one kid yelled, "and see how long you last without Big Daddy."

They all watched from the window as their evil neighbor emerged from his house with a blanket and some food for the sick child. This confused the children and they were

tempted to join their exiled brother when suddenly, Big
Daddy appeared. He roughly pulled his child from the
clutches of evil and proceeded to beat the wicked neighbor
senseless.

"Keep your filthy hands off this child!" Big Daddy
screamed as his children cheered him on. The police
arrived and arrested the neighbor for kidnapping while Big
Daddy re-entered his home with his prodigal son.

"Children," Big Daddy stated, "your brother is home. He
was lured away by that clever animal next door."

"But now," the child interrupted, "I see how wrong I was.
Please take me back."

Big Daddy beamed proudly as all his skinny children
embraced him. He flexed his muscles in the mirror and
made sure his hair was in place.

THE END

one billion live on

one buck daily; four days earn

Sunday New York Times

Wish you were here

- Longjaw Cisco
- Deepwater Cisco
- Lake Ontario Kiyi
- Blackfin Cisco
- Yellowfin Cutthroat Trout
- Alvord Cutthroat Trout
- Silver Trout
- Maravillas Red Shiner
- Independence Valley Tui Chub
- Thicktail Chub
- Pahranagat Spinedace
- Phantom Shiner
- Bluntnose Shiner
- Las Vegas Dace
- Grass Valley Speckled Dace
- Clear Lake Splittail
- Snake River Sucker
- Harelip Sucker
- Tecopa Pupfish
- Shoshone Pupfish

Sophocles rides the N Train

Nobody walks in the subway anymore. I say this to myself but even in my own head, my voice sounds weary this early in the morning.

Look down in the New York City subway and you'll see feet. Lots and lots of feet. In high heels, sneakers, work boots, dress shoes, and casual loafers, the feet pounding on the filthy, century-old floor have one thing in common: they are moving quickly. If it's not an all-out sprint, it's at least a two-steps-at-a-time, get-the-hell-out-of-my-way stride. In the middle of it all, I try to maintain a more reasonable pace amidst enough jostling and bumping to please even the most diehard roller derby fanatic.

The prehistoric subway system of New York City was obviously designed well before anyone could have ever have dreamed of millions of riders each day. Still, in general, that imposing amount of straphangers could theoretically all fit without much fuss if humanity was further along in its glacially gradual evolutionary process. But, since we're stuck in the primitive confines of the early twenty-first century, illogic reigns supreme and the trains are a daily—but essentially unfunny—replay of the infamous (and over-rated) stateroom scene in the Marx Brothers' classic 1936 film, *A Night At The Opera*. I say "over-rated," because the Marxsters did infinitely more comical work but somehow, it is the stateroom that has become synonymous with their genius thanks to myriad film critics afraid to buck the system and be original.

Be that as it may, once all the comfortless plastic subway seats are *muy occupado*, Big Apple train riders regularly display a bizarre affinity for the doorway.and therein, my friends, lies the rub. As each frustrated passenger boards, they silently insist on standing within a foot or two of the same door from which they entered. Thus, the middle of the car is a veritable oasis of acreage—a convincing testimony to the concept of space, if you will—but rarely does anyone even consider venturing beyond their beloved doorway. The inescapable aftermath of this irrational behavior as the train begins to get more and more crowded is, of course, serious human gridlock.

The preventable logjam by the door can get ugly. *Very* ugly. You have hundreds of frenzied rush hour commuters who—at this precise moment—pretty much hate their lives and their jobs. Yet, for some unexplain-able reason, they insist on standing in the most crowded portion of the car: the doorway.

It doesn't get much better on the stairs. As I deboard the N Train to walk down to the #5, I am greeted by another bottleneck, as it were. The pristine logic of one line of drones walking down and one line walking up is not within the grasp of Gotham's subway commuters. If I ever required evidence as to how humanity creates more problems than it could ever dream of solving, I need only stand back and witness the behavior on the Lexington Avenue staircase on your average weekday morning.

As I find myself an unwilling participant in this underground mosh pit, I can hear my man Sophocles chuckling as he sez: "The keenest sorrow is to recognize ourselves as the sole cause of all our adversities."

That goes double at rush hour…

No innocent bystanders in America

The next time you're feeling "free," see how far you can walk without being legally compelled to stop...to let cars drive past. The light turns red and viola: you are no longer free to continue walking because in America, the car culture rules. This essentially invisible totalitarian salvo was recently complicated when a big white SUV crept up into the crosswalk, making it virtually hopeless for yours truly to cross the damn street even when the light changed to green. I fixed my gaze on the mechanized monster before me and immediately saw all that is wrong with America.

No, I'm not just talking about how the gas guzzling properties of that SUV directly result in military interventions, human rights violations, global poverty, rampant war crimes, and everything else on that lurid laundry list. This is not just another screed about the myriad highways that crisscross America, draining tax dollars, shattering communities, and devastating eco-systems. No, this is all about dissidents finally blaming everyone who deserves blame (including ourselves).

The neatly dressed man in the passenger seat ("Dad") was talking loudly on a cell phone. Global demand for columbite-tantalite (a.k.a. "coltan"), a common cell phone component, is fueling war and environmental destruction in the Democratic Republic of Congo...but leftists aren't supposed to acknowledge their complicity. We don't reproach everyday Americans for their callous indifference because, well...it's all Bush's fault, right?

The woman driving this death machine ("Mom") sported diamond earrings. Although we're aware how the diamond trade exploits both humans and the landscape, Mom's given a free pass based solely on her ignorance. It's Bush's fault.

Both Mom and Dad proudly call themselves "liberal" and voted for Kerry in 2004. Their participation in the two-party farce and their acceptance of lesser evilism, however, are not seen as the problem by those in the know. It's all Bush's fault.

In the backseat of that SUV sat a teenage boy wearing Nike sneakers, a Gap shirt, and eating a Big Mac. I'm not supposed to point the accusing finger of blame at his family's willingness to financially support sweatshop labor and factory farming because it's Bush's fault.

Next to Big Mac boy was his older sister: drinking Coke (sorry India and Colombia) and putting on nail polish (too bad for the animals it was tested on). This girl's compliance is not the problem. She's merely a product of the times. Besides, it's all Bush's fault.

The light that temporarily halted this SUV went green and Mom put the pedal to the metal. As she drove away, I saw a bumper sticker that reads: "Our son is a U.S. Marine." Ah, here we have the Holy Grail of free passes. Condemn the war but support the troops, we're told, and the SUV owner's progeny only joined for the educational opportunities. It's not his fault. Leave him alone. He's only following orders. He had no choice. He has no culpability. It's Bush's fault that poor sonny boy is stuck in Iraq.

Reality check: The excuse of ignorance is not valid when graphic images are available within minutes. It's not lack of knowledge; it's denial...or perhaps even acquiescence.

There are no innocent bystanders when our money and/or rhetoric support the world's most powerful military and the corporate status quo. But if we just keep telling ourselves it's all Bush's fault, we can sleep better—our innocence wrapped around us like a big white SUV.

Stanley Milgram sez: "With numbing regularity, good people were seen to knuckle under the demands of authority and perform actions that were callous and severe. Men who are in everyday life responsible and decent were seduced by the trappings of authority, by the control of their perceptions, and by the uncritical acceptance of the experimenter's definition of the situation, into performing harsh acts. A substantial proportion of people do what they are told to do, irrespective of the content of the act and without limitations of conscience, so long as they perceive that the command comes from a legitimate authority."

Confession

Wouldn't want to be 18 years old today...what a mess we've made. Reminds me of something from *Fight Club*: "For thousands of years, human beings had screwed up and trashed and crapped on this planet, and now history expected me to clean up after everyone"

If only the promise of the 1960s wasn't co-opted, sanitized and sold back to us as a trend...if only we didn't buy into the one-size-fits-all commodity culture...if only we could see past the next fiscal quarter

If only I didn't take so long to wake the fuck up. Now. the point of no return is fading in the rearview mirror.

My apologies...

Mickey Z. sez: "There is one primary difference between Democrats and Republicans: they tell different lies to get elected."

The evolution will be televised (and maybe podcast, too)

"Loyalty to a petrified opinion never yet broke a chain or freed a human soul."

—Mark Twain

Observation. There is perhaps no more valuable tool in the world of science. Ask Darwin. He did all right for himself observing finches, didn't he? Or ask Marcel Proust. The writer everyone pretends to read said: "The true voyage of discovery lies not is seeking new landscapes but in having new eyes."

What I've recently observed with my very own "new eyes" is an expeditious evolution defying all previous postulations on how quickly a species can mutate, adapt, and evolve. In terms of daily habits, it's obvious from even the most tertiary scrutiny that *Homo sapiens* have undergone a fair amount of evolution, since 1945 or so. Thus, it is in the spirit of open-minded observers—from Galileo to Stephen Colbert—that I some elementary observations:

Humans, thanks to rapid-fire evolution, are no longer vulnerable to toxins. The mere act of perusing a typical American drink tap water (heavy metals and microbes), light up a cigarette (tar and nicotine), chat on a cell phone (electromagnetic radiation), chow down on a candy bar (sugar and chemicals) and an un-organic piece of fruit (pesticides and GMOs), wash it down with a glass of milk (animal protein, BGH, sub-therapeutic levels of antibiotics, and more pesticides), wipe her or his face with a napkin (chlorine and dyes), and then head off in a car (exhaust emissions) to the dentist for X-rays and a filling (radiation and mercury), is evidence enough for me. After all, would an entire nation so readily embrace such comportment as normal if it might hurt us?

With the recent surge in cell phones, beepers, palm pilots, Blackberries, and the like, isn't it safe to assume that human beings have evolved to become far more important now than they were 20 years ago?

Look around you: There are televisions in your gym, in your doctor's waiting room, in the Laundromat, airport, and every room of your house. Could it be that we simply need, on a physiological level, more stimulus than our ancestors did?

Speaking of TVs, if you combine the omnipresence of the television set with the ever-growing popularity of the Internet and the widespread utilization of iPod-style stereos, is it not logical to postulate that the early twenty-first century model human needs far less face-to-face social contact than its primitive, more chatty predecessors?

One more TV-related observation: Are televisions, automobiles, escalators, and elevators proof that the necessity for exercise and physical activity has gone the way of the dinosaur?

Walk into your bathroom. Walk into anyone's bathroom for that matter, and what do you see? A medicine chest, of course. Clearly, thanks to evolution, our immune systems have been relieved of the tedious chore of keeping us healthy. That task has been delegated to the wonders of modern science.

Can you explain why human beings behave in such a manner as to increase global warming and the greenhouse effect, promote the destruction of the ozone layer and the rain forests, and allow pollution to overtake many urban areas? To me, it's easy. Our superior bodies now require higher temperatures and less oxygen.

Now, if only some sectors of our species could simply evolve past the need for poverty, we'd really be in business.

Saving Condi's Life

There's a disturbing dynamic that occurs on every Manhattan street corner, every minute of every day. By simply watching the typical New York City pedestrian when he or she reaches the corner at a red light, you get a pretty good idea of what it's like to deal with an overcrowded, rancorous metropolitan area on a daily basis. *No one waits on the sidewalk.*

Even if a thousand cars are racing by, practically every single New Yorker insists on stepping a few steps out into the street while waiting for the light to change. They'll even go as far as squeezing themselves past other impatient street-crossers just to get to the front of the pack. We are so hyped up, so overstressed, so programmed to do everything fast that we can't even endure waiting 30 seconds for a damn traffic light. We'll risk death by stepping off the curb in order to get a head start on the green light.

With this in mind, here's a little thought experiment: Let's say I'm on such a corner as a pedestrian pushes past me— too harried to realize that she is stepping directly into the path of an oncoming SUV. I reach out, grab hold of her jacket, and yank her back to safety…only to realize it was none other than Condoleezza Rice. I wonder: *How might that make me feel?*

Initially, I hope I'd be gratified to have saved someone's life—even if that someone is responsible, in part, for many thousands of deaths (and counting). Given a few minutes to digest the scenario, I might begin to feel strange. What if I would've known in advance it was Rice whose life was in danger? Would I have risked bodily harm to save her? Condi Rice, in my estimation, is a terrible destructive force, part of the larger culture of destruction. I oppose the death penalty and thus do not wish Rice and her ilk to be removed via state sponsored murder, yet saving her life (or the life of any other major political/corporate player) is, by definition, to doom countless others to misery and death.

If I didn't react swiftly to pull Condi to safety, surely her passing would cause sadness. Friends and family would mourn. People would understandably be devastated, heartbroken. However, Rice's efforts have spread sorrow and mourning on a far greater scale. Has she ever considered the family and friends whose lives have been shattered thanks to her handiwork? Perhaps not, for it was Condoleezza Rice who once opined: "There is nothing wrong with doing something that benefits all humanity, but that is, in a sense, a second-order effect." It's not fantasy to assume that, across the globe, more folks would be celebrating than weeping if we lost the Secretary of State.

Still, of course, she's replaceable (just ask Rummy). There's always another commissar ready to step in and keep the machine running…with or without Condi. Thus, even those most vehemently opposed to American imperialism and interventionism would theoretically not even notice the change. I return to an earlier question: If I would've known in advance it was Condoleezza Rice whose life was in danger, would I have risked bodily harm to save her? On purely human terms, I think I would. What would you do?

"Those in power are poisoning children"
(Mussels not flexed?)

According to a study presented at the recent national meeting of the American Chemical Society, "remnants of Prozac are flushed from the body and travel in wastewater that reaches streams and rivers ... (and) cause female mussels to release their larvae before they're able to survive on their own." Tell this to the person sitting in the next cubicle and the typical response will likely be either indifference or bemusement. After all who gives a damn about a mussel?

This got me thinking about Rachel Carson, who with the publication of her book, *Silent Spring,* sounded a toxic wakeup call in 1962. "Can anyone believe it is possible to lay down such a barrage of poison on the surface of the earth without making it unfit for all life? " Carson asked 44 years ago. "They should not be called 'insecticides' but 'biocides.'"

Silent Spring simultaneously alerted the public to the chemical dangers all around them while incurring the predictable wrath of corporate America. Indeed, an author can be certain about his or her impact when companies like Monsanto—the good folks who brought us Agent Orange—take aim.

The use and abuse of pesticides, herbicides, and fungicides, Carson posited, were directly responsible for myriad health hazards not only for humans, but all life on the planet. "If the Bill of Rights contains no guarantee that a citizen shall be secure against lethal poisons distributed either by private individuals or by public officials," she wrote, "it is surely because our forefathers...could conceive of no such problem."

"*Silent Spring* showed that people are not master of nature, but rather part of nature," says Carson's biographer, John Henricksson. "It was a revolutionary thought at the time. Today no one seriously questions its truth, but in 1962 it was a direct attack on the values and assumptions of a society."

We could use some of that "revolutionary thought" stuff today as we now produce pesticides at a rate more than 13,000 times faster than we did in 1962. The Environmental Protection Agency—hardly a bulwark against corporate domination—considers 30 percent of all insecticides, 60 percent of all herbicides, and 90 percent of all fungicides to be carcinogenic, yet Americans spend about $7 billion on 21,000 different pesticide products each year.

"Prior to World War II, annual worldwide use of pesticides ran right around zero," says author Derrick Jensen. "By now it's 500 billion tons, increasing every year." As a result, about 860 Americans suffer from pesticide poisoning every single day; that's almost 315,000 cases per year. Some of the many symptoms of pesticide poisoning include: altered personality, memory loss, difficulty concentrating, dizziness, headaches, hyperactivity in children, wheezing cough, liver damage, kidney damage, constipation/diarrhea, decreased sex drive, decreased sperm count, severe muscle weakness, and cancer. The worldwide death rate from pesticide poisonings is more than 200,000 per year.

It's so, so easy to ignore or even mock the plight of mussel larvae but this is a canary in a coalmine situation. Those larvae are the mussel's children and what happens to them—in its own way—is happening to human children. "Let's be clear," Jensen concludes. "Those in power are poisoning children, stealing their physical and cognitive health: making them weak, sick, and stupid."

No wonder the whole damn planet is on Prozac.

Wish you were here

- Schomburgk's Deer
- Bonin Grosbeak
- Kona Grosbeak
- Ryukyu Pigeon
- Bonin Wood Pigeon
- Big Thicket Hog-nosed Skunk
- Rabbit-eared Tree-rat
- White-footed Tree-rat
- Carolina Parakeet
- New Zealand Quail
- Raiatea Parakeet
- Black-fronted Parakeet
- Chatham Island Swan
- Western quoll
- Brawny Great Moa
- Philippine Bare-backed Fruit Bat
- King Island Emu
- Kangaroo Island Emu
- Falkland Island Wolf
- Passenger Pigeon

Blame it on the Comet

Sixty-five million years ago, a plucky little planet named
Earth was braving the third period of the Mesozoic Age.
The first period was Triassic; then came the Spielberg...I
mean, Jurassic (and you can bet your Jurassic, it was far
more amazing than any computer-generated version). The
third period was none other than the Cretaceous. Many
scientists believe that during the Cretaceous Period, a
colossal comet (or conceivably an asteroid)—perhaps 10
kilometers across—impacted upon what is now commonly
accepted as the Yucatán Peninsula of Mexico with the
force of 100 million hydrogen bombs. It left behind a
crater 112 miles wide and 3,000 feet deep.

The resulting tsunami and subsequent impact winter, so
goes the theory, wiped out 50-80% of all plants and
animals—including a flourishing species at the pinnacle of
the food chain: Dinosaurs. The sudden absence of massive
reptilian predators allowed for the eventual emergence of a
little something I like to call "Homo sapiens." (That's us,

for those of you scoring at home.) In other words, if you agree than we humans have not exactly been the most responsible species, well, there's a giant comet to blame.

I know what some of you are thinking: Surely, Mickey Z., humans aren't as dangerous as a T. Rex, right? To them, I ask: In all the millions of years dinosaurs roamed this planet, did any of them feel the need to invent, say, nuclear weapons? Is there a single stegosaurus responsible for conducting secret nuclear experiments on its own species? Nope, it took humanity to think up an idea like this:

Shortly after the nuking of civilians at Hiroshima and Nagasaki, U.S. researchers set about, at any cost, to discern the effects of plutonium on the human body. "There were two kinds of experiments," says Peter Montague, director of the Environmental Research Foundation. "In one kind, specific small groups (African-American prisoners, mentally retarded children, and others) were induced, by money or by verbal subterfuge, to submit to irradiation of one kind or another. In all, some 800 individuals participated in these 'guinea pig' trials. In the second kind, large civilian populations were exposed to intentional releases of radioactive isotopes into the atmosphere."

When word of these tests leaked in 1993, another solely

human creation—the corporate media—stepped up to the plate with justifications like this from *Newsweek*: "The scientists who had conducted those tests so long ago surely had rational reasons: the struggle with the Soviet Union, the fear of imminent nuclear war, the urgent need to unlock all the secrets of the atom, for purposes both military and medical." But this was no momentary lapse in judgment. This was and has always been standard operating procedure for the planet's dominant species. After all, the declassified documents on U.S. radiation experiments stretch three miles long.

Even today's "monsters" are far less harmful than we "intelligent" humans. No great white shark created pesticides, napalm, Agent Orange, or the internal combustion engine; you can't blame cigarettes, greenhouse gases, hydroelectric dams, or mercury-laced vaccinations on a pit bull; and rest assured no non-human conjured up zoos, animal experimentation, or the circus.

Clearly, if *Homo sapiens* have put all earthly life at risk, there's only direction in which to aim the accusing finger of culpability. In your next moment of human-induced fury, frustration, commiseration, or despair, endeavor a fresh perspective and blame it on the comet.

Top Ten Ways to Plan Your Next Anti-War Protest

1. Hold it on a weekend day so it doesn't interfere with most work and school schedules

2. Be sure to properly request your permit

3. Don't invite the anarchists

4. Ask Jesse Jackson, Susan Sarandon, and Michael Moore to speak

5. Costumes!

6. Agree in advance with authorities as to how many protestors are willing to be arrested

7. Invite a broad multi-culti mix to present the illusion of a coalition

8. Bring lots of "Support the Troops" signs

9. Puppets!

10. Contact United for Peace & Justice and/or International ANSWER and follow their orders...I mean, advice

This woman really wanted people to stare at her chest

A woman walks into the gym...no, this is not the opening line to a joke. The woman enters the gym wearing a very tight blue t-shirt bearing the images of George H.W. Bush and George W. Bush across her chest. Under the two war criminals are the words: "Dumb and Dumber."

The woman has customized this shirt by cutting off the sleeves and turning a crew neck into a v-neck. The "V" she has created plunged low...down to cleavage level. A Bush smiles at me blankly from either side the V's lowest point.

Most gym members are far too engrossed in their curls, crunches, and calorie burning to notice this subversive in their midst, but more than a few folks do stare at her shirt...including yours truly. Here's some of what I am thinking as I do:

The shirt's message is counterproductive to genuine change because it indirectly suggests that we'd all be better off with a Democrat in the White House if for no other reason than a Democrat would more acceptable to us in the educated class. The system works just fine, thank you, it's just that the wrong person's in charge.

Neither Bush the Elder or Bush the Lesser is anywhere near "dumb" in the sense the shirt's message suggests. Let me first clarify that, of course, every single one of us is incredibly "dumb" because we perpetuate behavior that we each know will eventually destroy us and much of life on the planet. But the use of the word "dumb" on this woman's t-shirt implies that members of the Bush family are simply not intelligent enough to handle the duties of the presidency and thus the atrocities committed during their watch can be merely chalked up to low IQ. Again, let's not get worked up enough to change anything more than which party has placed a figurehead at the top.

Dissent (*sic*) is merely a commodity and has been for a long, long time. Radicalism is a t-shirt, a bumper sticker, a hairstyle, a ribbon pinned on a lapel, or maybe even the occasional march or protest. Activism for most of us is a spectacle with little or no foundation or duration. In 2006 America, we prove our rebel status by wearing a message t-shirt while walking on the goddamned Stairmaster...our eyes transfixed on the little television attached to the exercise machine. Surely, the members of America's elite class are quaking in their overpriced boots.

That woman's t-shirt has likely garnered her many knowing smiles and nods as she stands in line at Starbuck's and started a few friendly arguments in the parking lot at IKEA. That's democracy and freedom for you. We can wear our opinions on a shirt without fear of being tossed in a gulag (well, as long as the shirt doesn't promote something un-American like anarchy). We can disagree with fellow citizens over which rich white male should live in the White House for the next four years...but still remain united in our love for our country. We can speak out against any war started by the party we don't like but we always support "our" troops. That's just how things are in the land of the free and that's precisely why "they" hate us so much.

If only "they" had the freedom to wear a message t-shirt with a plunging neckline, the world would be a much safer place.

slavery: a capitalist parable

in the most remote regions of brazil, slave labor is

employed to cut down grand swaths of the precious rain

forest to make room to grow eucalyptus which is then

burned by male slaves (who exploit the body, mind, and

spirit of female slaves forced into prostitution) to make

charcoal for the steel mills of brazil where the poorest of

the poor toil for wages that do not sustain them so that

steel can be shipped to a general motors plant in mexico

(gm is now the second largest employer south of the

border) where the poorest of the poor endure *maquiladora*

conditions so these automobile parts can then be shipped

to a gm plant in the u.s. (roughly 50 percent of what is

termed "trade" consists of business transactions between

branches of the same transnational corporation) where

even the poorest of the poor proudly take on imposing

debt to possess a car "made in the u.s.a." so they can clog

the highways that were paved over inestimable eco-
systems, filling the air with noxious pollution as they make
their way to the drive-through window of an anti-union
fast food restaurant that purchased the beef of slaughtered
cattle that once grazed on land cleared by male slaves who
exploit the body, mind, and spirit of female slaves in the
most remote regions of brazil.

Wish you were here

- Puerto Rican Shrew
- Puerto Rican Long-nosed Bat
- Puerto Rican Long-tongued Bat
- Guam Flying Fox
- Penasco Chipmunk
- Pallid Beach Mouse
- Atlantic Gray Whale
- Kenai Peninsula Wolf
- Newfoundland Wolf
- Banks Island Wolf
- Cascade Mountains Wolf
- Northern Rocky Mountain Wolf
- Mogollon Mountain Wolf
- Texas Gray Wolf
- Southern Rocky Mountain Wolf
- Florida Red Wolf
- Texas Red Wolf
- California Grizzly Bear
- Tacoma Pocket Gopher

Bob Dylan sez: "Democracy don't rule the world. You'd better get that in your head. This world is ruled by violence. But I guess that's better left unsaid."

Pop Quiz

Q. Who gave up a life of luxury and turned his back on millions to fight in the mountains and caves of Afghanistan for what he believed in and, as a result, is revered by millions as a "hero"?

A. Osama bin Laden.

(Alternate answer: Pat Tillman)

Stillborn

(a poem of occupation)

Somewhere...

in the backstreets of Mosul

(or maybe Falluja)

it happens like a

meteor streaking across the

pre-dawn horizon

An Iraqi girl or (as she'd rather be called) teen...

standing before a window

conjures

a new thought

Something never before conceptualized

The sort of notion that, if nurtured and respected,

might alter the course of human history

Before she can savor more than three

seconds of epiphany...before her eyes can even display

the joy of revelation,

she is mistaken for an "insurgent"

(or was it "terrorist"?)

Sun begins to rise

Rays of light shoot through

bullet holes in her tattered window shade

The girl takes her last breath

as yet another day begins

Can we be anti-war but pro-troops?

For some, the phrase "support our troops" is merely a euphemism for: support the policies that put the troops there in the first place. For others—including many activists—the mantra is a safe way to avoid taking an unqualified, uncompromising stand against this war (and *all* war). Many who identify themselves as "anti-war" still vigorously defend the troops…no questions asked.

The excuse making typically falls into two broad categories. The first being: "Our troops are just following orders."

A simple Web search will find many reasons why this concept has no legal basis. For example, Principle IV of Nuremberg Tribunal (1950) states: "The fact that a person acted pursuant to order of his government or of a superior does not relieve him from responsibility under international law provided a moral choice was in fact possible to him."

Besides this, it can be easily posited that "only following orders" also has no moral footing. Of course, the facile example would be Nazi Germany. But surely every suicide bomber is merely following orders as are those detonating IEDs in Iraq. The Left praised Vietnam era draftees who fled to Canada. Yet, today's volunteer warriors are given a free pass because they didn't give the orders in an illegal war and occupation. This is not only illegal and immoral; it also lacks any radical credibility. Somehow, individuals and groups can stand tall against war and military intervention but refuse to shine a light on those who choose (and get paid) to fight. Nowhere else in the realm of activism does such a paradox exist.

Consider the animal rights activists struggling to end the morally indefensible and scientifically fraudulent enterprise of animal experimentation. Can they expose the corporations and academic institutions but somehow "support" the actual scientists performing the lab experiments? Surely, they are "just doing their job" and "following orders."

How about those fighting to end unfair labor practices? Is it acceptable to call out the CEOs of Nike & The Gap but hang yellow ribbons for those who handle day-to-day operations of a sweatshop in, say, Vietnam? These men and women are just as "stuck in a bad situation" as any grunt in Iraq or Afghanistan.

The second excuse usually sounds like this: "It's a poverty draft. These poor souls have to enlist because they any economic options." America is certainly an unjust economic society and this would be a compelling argument...if it were true. A 2006 *New York Times* op-ed highlighted a study by Tim Kane and Mackenzie Eaglen that "analyzed demographic data on every single enlistee, not just a sample, and found that in terms of education, last year's recruits were just as qualified as those of any recent year, and maybe the best ever. Over all, wartime recruits since 1999 are in many respects comparable to the youth population on the whole, except that they are on average a bit wealthier, much more likely to have graduated from high school and more rural than their civilian peers." They also found that youths "from wealthy American ZIP codes are volunteering in ever higher numbers" while "enlistees from the poorest fifth of American neighborhoods fell nearly a full percentage point over the last two years, to 13.7 percent. In 1999, that number was exactly 18 percent."

So, are some of the soldiers in Iraq there primarily for economic reasons? *Sure.* Did others sign up for a chance to shoot some "ragheads"? *Probably.* After factoring out these two relatively small groups and rejecting the illegal, immoral, and reactionary "only following orders" defense, I ask this of anti-war activists: Exactly how are the men and women who willingly signed up to wage war in Iraq and Afghanistan immune from any and all scrutiny and/or blame?

After all, what do you think "our troops" are doing? "We know that 99.9% of our forces conduct themselves in an exemplary manner," says Donald Rumsfeld. "We also know that in conflicts things that shouldn't happen do happen."

If only 1/10 of 1% of US soldiers make "things happen that shouldn't happen," what are the rest doing to have us standing and singing "God Bless America" during the 7th inning stretch at Yankee Stadium? How do we define *exemplary manner?*

By Rumsfeld's reckoning (and the standard company line of most every politician, pundit, and peon) "exemplary" includes (among other things) the use of Daisy Cutters, cluster bombs, napalm, depleted uranium, white phosphorus, and the launching cruise missiles into crowded cities.

"Things that shouldn't happen do happen," Rumsfeld explains. But what about all the stuff that this society accepts "should" happen? Why would anyone besides a sadist feel compelled to *support* that unconditionally?

There are two powerful myths/ironies propping up the "support the troops" premise. The first involves what they are doing in Iraq and Afghanistan in the first place. I can't tell you how many e-mails I've received over the years that read something like this: "While you sit at home in your luxurious apartment, making money off your writing (*insert laugh track here*), those brave men and women are putting their asses on the line to fight for your freedom to write your anti-American garbage.

I say: *Bullshit.*

The troops in Iraq and Afghanistan are not fighting for my freedom. They are fighting to keep the world safe for petroleum. If anything, since 9/11, our freedom has been slowly eroded and the presence of the US military in Iraq and Afghanistan makes it harder for anyone to speak up in dissent. If I were in an airport, and I spoke aloud what I've written in this article, I'd likely be detained or arrested.

Irony #2: While most American citizens are manipulated, harassed, coerced, and guilted into hanging yellow ribbons—even if they're anti-war—from Shays Rebellion in 1787 to Coxey's Army to the Bonus Army to the Gulf War Syndrome to a quarter-million homeless vets today, generation after generation of US military personnel has suffered a lack of support from their own government (and the corporations that own it). "Our troops" are just as controlled and exploited as the US citizens that worship them.

And one more thing: Let's stop with the "our troops" charade. You and I may foot the bill, but "we" have no say in what they do. If those truly were "my" men and women,

I'd bring them right home and put them to work doing something useful...like turning the Long Island Expressway into the world's longest organic farm.

Don't support the troops...*inform them.*

And one more thing: Let's stop with the "our troops" charade. You and I may foot the bill, but "we" have no say in what they do. If those truly were "my" men and women, I'd bring them right home and put them to work doing something useful...like turning the Long Island Expressway into the world's longest organic farm.

Al Sharpton sez: "If you piss on my face, I'm not gonna call it rain."

Ward Churchill: Poet?

To me, the following quote reads like a poem...so that's how I'll present it:

You've got to learn

that when you push people around,

some people push back.

As they should.

As they must.

And as they undoubtedly will.

There is justice in such symmetry.

—Ward Churchill

All you need is love

…and a small, well-trained army

Why I support the "War on Terror"

Yes, I support the "War on Terror." No, I'm not declaring
public allegiance to the current jihad against a tactic (which
is in actuality a war against terrorist attacks not perpetrated
by the United States or its allies/client states)...I'm thinking
of another meaning entirely for our new favorite word:
"terror."

As defined at Dictionary.com, "an overwhelming feeling of
fear and anxiety" and/or an "intense, overpowering fear"
characterize the brand of terror I speak of. Don Lutz,
author of *The First Ism*, has written that such "terror" is
"what one feels when being kidnapped or raped." Lutz
goes on to list other terrifying examples:

> Terror is what poor people worldwide feel when
> approached by uniformed, armed men; what animals feel in
> research laboratories; what people feel when their families
> are faced with starvation; what a child feels when an adult
> starts to hit; what millions of families feel when they hear

planes overhead; what fish feel when hooked in the mouth; what people fell under threat of having loved ones tortured or killed; what forest dwellers feel when the loggers come in to clear-cut; what people feel when they are threatened with invasion; and what animals feel at slaughterhouses.

You want to wage war against terror, why not find a worthy adversary? No need for shady FBI stings, unconstitutional wire tapping, or panic-inducing color-coded warnings that conveniently pop up at the most politically expedient intervals; the variety of terror described by Lutz above is genuine and it's endemic. Perhaps a big step toward ending the use of terror as a tactic would be to alleviate the feeling of terror triggered across the globe by the home of the brave.

It's noteworthy that so many Americans reflexively defend their (*sic*) country's rampant illegalities because they perceive these actions as falling under the seductive justification of "defending our way of life." But, if our way of life is so sacred, so ideal, so worthy of being defended by any means necessary...why are millions of us reeling from "intense, overpowering fear"? If the U.S. represents a superior form of society, why do we need so many homeless shelters, alcohol and drug rehab centers, rape crisis hotlines, battered women's shelters, prisons, law enforcement agents, and soldiers? Why does a sexual assault occur every two and a half minutes? If the United States of America is the world's shining light, why are its citizens compelled to organize movements to protect human, environmental, and animal rights? Why can't we drink the water or breathe the air without risking our health? Why do we experience "intense, overpowering fear" about being made ill by corporate-produced toxins and having no health insurance to deal with such an illness? If America is the zenith of human social order, why does its very name evoke "an overwhelming feeling of fear and anxiety" for people both here and abroad? Why does our vaunted "way of life" provoke terror both as a tactic and an emotion?

People just love to hear themselves say: "We're fighting to preserve our way of life." The U.S. constitutes roughly 5% of the earth's population but consumes about 25% of the earth's resources. Maybe "our way of life" makes us the real terrorists.

With the point of no return fading in the rearview mirror (or at least obscured by an SUV), the time is long overdue for all of us to recognize the real enemy is that which inspires terror...as in "an overwhelming feeling of fear and anxiety" and/or an "intense, overpowering fear."

Dumb and Dumbo
(One act, two parties)

The action takes place in a NYC police station on a Saturday afternoon in the present day.

Characters:

NYPD DETECTIVE DUMBO—male, late 30s

NYPD OFFICER MULE—male, early 30s

JOHNNY VOTER—male, early 20s

AT RISE: As the lights go up, we see Dumbo, Mule, and Johnny in a locked room. A very nervous Johnny is seated at a table.

MULE: *(to Dumbo)* So, what we got here?

DUMBO: One of them punks from today's protests. Him and his pals think they have something to important say and it's okay to break the law to say it.

With that, Dumbo delivers a hard slap to the back of Johnny's head.so hard that Dumbo shakes his hand in pain afterwards.

MULE: *(to Dumbo)* You okay?

DUMBO: I'll be fine. Ain't no protest punk that can hurt me. They're powerless.

Mule moves to the far corner of the room as Dumbo closes in on Johnny.

DUMBO: *(to Johnny)* You're fucked, kid. I hope you know that. We know all about your plans. All that's left is find out who else was in on it.

JOHNNY: Plans?

Dumbo lands another smack to the kid's head and again appears to have hurt his hand.

MULE: *(to Dumbo)* You better be careful.

DUMBO: *(to Mule)* You think I'm out of line?

MULE: I meant you better be careful or might break your hand on his head.

DUMBO: *(to Johnny)* Wise up, punk. We know you and your anarchist buddies wanted to smash that Starbucks' window. You think we don't know things? We hear your phone calls, we read your e-mails, we can see right into your friggin' head if we want to.

JOHNNY: We just wanted to buy coffee. We were cold.

DUMBO: Cold? You want cold? *(laughs)* Wait till you spend a few nights at Rikers.

JOHNNY: I want to see my lawyer.

This brings a big smile to Dumbo's face. He starts to laugh and looks over at Mule but Mule is too busy checking himself in a small mirror. Dumbo yanks the chair from under Johnny.sending the kid to the hard floor.

DUMBO: Give us names, punk, or you'll be in no condition to see a lawyer. The law can't help you now because I *am* the law.

Mule walks over to Dumbo.

MULE: Take a break, Dumbo. Let me give it a shot.

DUMBO: I'll give you ten minutes, Mule. After that, I'm taking off the gloves. We're going Gitmo on his ass.

Dumbo storms out as Mule helps the kid back into his chair.

MULE: I don't like his style any more than you do.

JOHNNY: Then why didn't you do something?

MULE: You don't understand. My hands are tied. But now we can do this the right way.

JOHNNY: He'll be back in ten minutes.

MULE: It won't take you that long to give me a few names so we can get you home for dinner.

JOHNNY: I don't want any trouble.

MULE: I can see that, kid. Tell me who really set this up and you'll be fine. Trust me.

JOHNNY: *(starts to cry)* But...

MULE: Hey, when Dumbo gets back, all bets are off.
Guys like him are different than us. You gotta trust me...
comrade.

Johnny nods his head. Mule hands him a pen and a small notebook. A sobbing Johnny scribbles down names as Dumbo returns. Mule looks up at Dumbo and winks.

DUMBO: Mission accomplished.

Freedom is deafening

Once upon a time...I was eating lunch in a Virginia Beach diner with bunch of friends when we heard a deafening roar.

"What was that?" I bellowed.

Our waitress smiled and proudly replied: "That's an F-14 ...the sound of freedom."

Intermission

Perhaps the most outstanding conclusion of such a study is that [Lee Harvey] Oswald was profoundly alienated from the world in which he lived. His life was characterized by isolation, frustration, and failure. He had very few, if any, close relationships with other people and appeared to have great difficulty in finding a meaningful place in the world. . [His wife] Marina Oswald thought that he would not be happy anywhere, "Only on the moon, perhaps."

(From *The Warren Commission Report*)

Self-Help in the Land of Denial

Legend has it that the song "Sexy Sadie" was written as a response to what the Beatles experienced while getting Zenny with their one-time guru, Maharishi Mahesh Yogi. Accusations of sexual indiscretions led to John Lennon and George Harrison dismissing the Maharishi as a fraud. Subsequently, Lennon wrote "Sexy Sadie," originally called, "Maharishi, Maharishi What Have You Done." Harrison, so the story goes, convinced Lennon to change the title...and years later, there is still much dispute over the veracity of the Beatles' charges against Maharishi. The tragic human need for gurus did not diminish after the Beatles' dalliance or the release of "Sexy Sadie."

"We do not naturally aspire to any hazy, narcotic Nirvana, where our critical and ironic faculties would be of no use to us," writes Christopher Hitchens.

Imagine a state of endless praise and gratitude and adoration, as the Testaments ceaselessly enjoin us to do, and you have conjured a world of hellish nullity and conformism.

Contrary to Hitchens' reality check, guru-mania has today reached epidemic proportions. If you don't believe me, check out the "self-help" section in any bookstore.

How privileged are we? How self-centered is the American book reader? The world's 587 billionaires are worth $1.9 trillion—a total higher than the gross domestic product of the 170 poorest countries combined—yet our bookshelves are creaking under the weight of innumerable books exhorting us to dwell in denial: if we all simply stayed positive, everything would be fine.

Tell it to the little Thai girl...sold into slavery by her own dirt-poor parents so they could afford a television. Their flesh and blood raped and beaten into a life of prostitution for Japanese tourists until she contracts any number of diseases and gets kicked out of the brothel to die on the streets.

If we were to believe the meditation mafia, that poor misguided Thai girl simply needed a positive attitude. Maybe if she just read Anthony Robbins or went to Madonna's Kabbalah class, she'd also be able to connect

with her inner child and develop enough self-esteem to
sign a petition to free Tibet on her way to Pilates class in
the goddamned West Village.

Let's check the scorecard:

- 587 billionaires are worth more than 170 countries.
- Nearly 4 billion people around the world earn less
  than $1,500 a year.

What makes the American people so confident there isn't a
long overdue bill to be paid while they meditate, deviate,
and pontificate?

As the Indian-born author/activist Arundhati Roy
explains:

> People from poorer places and poorer countries have to call
> upon their compassion not to be angry with ordinary people
> in America.

Native American scholar Ward Churchill takes it
further...warning us that the same people Roy refers to

> have no obligation—moral, ethical, legal or otherwise—to
> sit on their thumbs while the opposition here dithers about
> doing anything to change the system.

Self-help authors are raking in royalties by capitalizing on capitalism's consequences while every two seconds, a child starves to death somewhere on Planet Earth. When all is said and done, I'll take Tupac over Deepak any day of the week.

Carl Sagan sez: "One of the saddest lessons of history is this: If we've been bamboozled long enough, we tend to reject any evidence of the bamboozle. We're no longer interested in finding out the truth. The bamboozle has captured us. It is simply too painful to acknowledge—even to ourselves—that we've been so credulous."

America the Temporary

Sigmund Freud sez: "America is gigantic; but a gigantic mistake."

America is a nation built upon myth. If you don't believe me, consider the Florentine merchant-adventurer after whom this country was named. Amerigo Vespucci probably made at least two voyages to the Americas, but he was not the leader of any expedition or the first European of his era to set foot on the mainland. (America named after a self-hyping fraud? It's just too perfect.) Yes, the USA is a nation built upon myth...and the greatest myth of all is that the land of the free is gonna last forever.

I'm sure the Aztecs, the Incas, the Romans, and the Mongols were pretty damn pleased with themselves and figured what they were doing could never end. Yet, like Percy Bysshe Shelley's "Ozymandias," they are ancient history. (Shelley and his brand of poetry, alas, are also

prehistoric.) The Ottoman Empire ran longer than *Cats*,
for chrissake, and all they left is a place to put your feet
after a long day of trading pork bellies.

America the Beautiful. The Declaration of Independence.
The Statue of Liberty. Baseball, apple pie, and internal
combustion engines called Chevrolet. All of these are
nothing more than the castles made of sand Jimi Hendrix
sang about. Hendrix, for that matter, is yet another
sandcastle. Take it even further: Eiffel Tower, Big Ben,
and, as *Fight Club's* Tyler Durden reminds us: "Even the
Mona Lisa's falling apart." Our denial forces us to ignore
this reality but, whether we admit it or not, what we call
"civilization," is indeed fleeting.

If you don't believe me, I have one word for you: Maya. If
one were to view that civilization from Pre-Mayan to Pre-
Columbian, it spanned roughly 3500 years before
collapsing. America is 230 years old. The Mayans had us
beat by more than 30 centuries but are now barely more
than a footnote for most humans. No one is certain what
happened to cause the demise of the Mayan culture but
this description from the One World Journeys website

(http://www.oneworldjourneys.com) has an jarringly
recognizable ring:

> History is a continual ebb and flow of civilizations, but the
> collapse of many great Maya cities occurred within a fairly
> short amount of time centuries before the Spanish arrived.
> Archeologists are still trying to answer the mystery of why
> this happened. Several answers are emerging, with
> overpopulation and the resulting exhaustion of land
> resources leading the list. The soil of the rain forest is
> actually poor in nutrients. Crops can be grown for only two
> or three years, then must be allowed to go fallow for up to
> 18 years. This requires ever increasing destruction of the
> rain forest (and animal habitat) to feed a growing
> population. Other reasons for the collapse include increased
> warfare; a prolonged drought; a bloated ruling class
> requiring more and more support from the worker classes;
> increased sacrifices extending even to the lower classes; and
> possible epidemics owing to the dense populations in the
> urban centers.

It calls to mind the words of jazz legend Sonny Rollins:
"What I am more concerned about is whether our whole
civilization will be around in the next 25 years."

Ashamed to be American

I was reading *Five Years of My Life: An Innocent Man in Guantanamo*, by Murat Kurnaz, when I came across a passage about Kurnaz being subjected to gruesome electric shock torture at the hands of America's brave volunteer warriors. After passing out and being tossed back in his cell to sleep it off, Kurnaz was soon awakened by harrowing screams.

He saw two valiant American soldiers hitting a man who was lying on the ground—his head wrapped in a blanket. Five more patriotic heroes eventually joined in on the beating, hitting the man's head with the butts of their rifles and kicking him with their heavy boots. "Then," says Kurnaz, "they walked away, leaving him lying there."

The next morning, the man was still lying in the same spot: in a pool of blood. It wasn't until later that afternoon that four US officers came to inspect him and an escort team earned their yellow ribbons by taking away his lifeless body.

"I wondered to myself if had any children," writes Kurnaz. "Whether his mother and father would ever find out that he had been beaten to death. At that moment, I didn't care whether it was him or me. My life was worth nothing more than his. I'd understood for quite some time what this camp was about. They could do with us what they pleased. And I might be next."

Even if the man who was beaten was death was proven— beyond a reasonable doubt—to be personally responsible for 9/11, how can anyone but a sociopath justify such treatment? Can anyone but a sadistic criminal justify the existence of "Gitmo"? How much more will it take before everyday Americans collectively hang their heads in shame over this ongoing crime and the many other examples of their (*sic*) nation's contemptible conduct?

Are any of you ashamed of the epidemics of preventable diseases like cancer, heart disease, diabetes, etc.? What about the poisoning of our air, water, and food (including mother's breast milk); the one-third of Americans uninsured or underinsured when it comes to health care; the fact that 61% of US corporations do not even pay taxes; the presidential lies, electoral fraud, limited debates, and so on; the largest prison population on the planet; corporate control of public land, public airwaves, public pensions; overt infringement of our civil liberties; bloated defense budget, unilateral military interventions, war crimes committed in our name, legalization of torture, blah blah blah?

What will it take before you are wholeheartedly ashamed to be American?

Ask yourself these two questions:

- Do I feel the planet is in peril?
- Do I believe that those in power—those most responsible for the planet being in peril—will relinquish power voluntarily?

If you answered "yes" to number one and "no" to number two, I have one more question for you: How much are you willing to endure before you take serious, sustained action?

A new type of criminal

In *Eichmann in Jerusalem*, Hannah Arendt wrote,

> The trouble with Eichmann was precisely that so many were like him, and that the many were neither perverted nor sadistic, that they were, and still are, terribly and terrifyingly normal.

She wrote of a "new type of criminal," who

> commits his crimes under circumstances that make it well-nigh impossible for him to know or to feel that he is doing wrong.

Raise your hand if this sounds frighteningly familiar.

Wish you were here

- Round combshell (clam)
- Tennessee Riffleshell (mussel)
- Sampson's Pearlymussel (Wabash Riffleshell)
- Epioblasma sampsonii
- Syrian Wild Ass
- Equus hemionus hemippus
- Burly Lesser Moa
- Arabian Gazelle
- Red Gazelle
- Saudi Gazelle
- Goff's Southeastern Pocket Gopher
- Confused Moth
- Steller's Sea Cow
- Lesser Stick-nest Rat
- Mauritius Grey Parrot
- Bavarian Vole
- Indian Seal
- Black-footed Ferret
- Lanai Thrush
- New Zealand Greater Short-tailed Bat

Why I hate America

"Why do you hate America?" This is a remarkably easy question to provoke. One might, for instance, expose elements of this nation's brutal foreign policy. Ask a single probing question about, say, U.S. complicity in the overthrow of governments in Guatemala, Iran, or Chile and thin-skinned patriots (*sic*) will come out of the woodwork to defend their country's honor by accusing you of being "anti-American." Of course, this allegation might lead me to ponder how totalitarian a culture this must be to even entertain such a concept, but I'd rather employ the vaunted Arundhati defense. The incomparable Ms. Roy says: "What does the term 'anti-American' mean? Does it mean you are anti-jazz or that you're opposed to freedom of speech? That you don't delight in Toni Morrison or John Updike? That you have a quarrel with giant sequoias?" (I'm a tree hugger remember? I don't argue with sequoias.)

When pressed, I sometimes reply: "I don't hate America. In fact, think it's one of the best countries anyone ever stole." But, after the laughter dies down, I have a confession to make: If by "America" they mean the elected/appointed officials and the corporations that own them, well, I guess I do hate that America—with justification.

Among many reasons, I hate America for the near-extermination and subsequent oppression of its indigenous population. I hate it for its role in the African slave trade and for dropping atomic bombs on civilians. I hate its control of institutions like the United Nations, World Bank, International Monetary Fund, and World Trade Organization. I hate it for propping up brutal dictators like Suharto, Pinochet, Duvalier, Hussein, Marcos, and the Shah of Iran. I hate America for its unconditional support for Israel. I hate its bogus two-party system, its one-size-fits-all culture, and its income gap. I could go on for pages but I'll sum up with this: I hate America for being a hypocritical white supremacist capitalist patriarchy.

After a paragraph like that, you know what comes next: If you hate America so much, why don't you leave? Leave

America? That would potentially put me on the other end of U.S. foreign policy. No thanks.

I like how Paul Robeson answered that question before the House Un-American Activities Committee in 1956:

> My father was a slave and my people died to build this country, and I'm going to stay right here and have a part of it, just like you. And no fascist-minded people like you will drive me from it. Is that clear?

Since none of my people died to build anything, I rely instead on William Blum, who declares,

> I'm committed to fighting U.S. foreign policy, the greatest threat to peace and happiness in the world, and being in the United States is the best place for carrying out the battle. This is the belly of the beast, and I try to be an ulcer inside of it.

Needless to say, none of the above does a damn thing to placate the yellow ribbon crowd. It seems what offends flag-wavers most is when someone like me makes use of the freedom they claim to adore. According to their twisted logic, I am ungrateful for my liberty if I have the audacity to exercise it. If I make the choice to not salute the flag during the seventh inning stretch at Yankee

Stadium, somehow I'm not worthy of having the freedom to make the choice to not salute the flag during the seventh inning stretch at Yankee Stadium. These so-called patriots not only claim to celebrate freedom while refusing my right to exploit it, they also ignore the social movements that fought for and won such freedoms.

There's plenty of tolerated public outcry against the Bush administration and the occupation of Iraq, but it's neither fashionable nor acceptable to go as far as saying, no, I do not support the troops and yes, I hate what America does. Fear of recrimination allows the status quo to control the terms of debate. Until we voice what is in our hearts and have the nerve to admit what we hate...we will never create something that can be loved.

Kurt Vonnegut sez: "Humans are a mistake. We have destroyed our entire planet."

"Philosophical differences"

When the FBI arrested several members (*sic*) of the Earth Liberation Front (ELF) in early 2006, it came as no surprise that much of the corporate media rejoiced. A fine example is an editorial that appeared in the *Seattle Post-Intelligencer* at the time. The ELF's alleged actions, the editors pronounced, challenged "society's ability to conduct itself peacefully" and demonstrated "arrogant, vicious thinking." Most notable is this declaration: "There's no philosophical difference between approving the torching of a large new home on Camano Island or the targeting of the tallest towers in Manhattan."

For the sake of argument, let's assume the *Seattle Post-Intelligencer* is correct in all of the above statements. What then, is the "philosophical difference" between the targeting of the tallest towers in Manhattan and the dropping of white phosphorous on babies in Iraq and why isn't the corporate media setting aside space to ponder that

question? Much is made of FBI claims that the ELF and
ALF (Animal Liberation Front) represent the greatest
domestic threat today but in the land that never
apologizes, anything goes in the name of waging war on a
tactic (terror).

Bringing it closer to home, one can only wonder if the
Seattle Post-Intelligencer perceives factory farming as a
challenge to "society's ability to conduct itself peace-fully"?
Do the editors believe the morally bankrupt and
scientifically fraudulent institution of animal experimentation demonstrates "arrogant, vicious thinking" or is such
a label reserved only for official enemies?

Some will support ELF methods while others will strongly
denounce them. In order to make such a determination,
however, we need facts not hyperbole and fortunately, not
all corporate media outlets issued a blanket condemnation
of the ELF. Dean Schabner of ABCNews.com explained
that the "majority of the postings on the ELF Web site
have maintained a commitment to avoiding injury to
people, even those responsible for the projects they
oppose." Schabner added: "They believe that the damage
being done to the Earth by pollution, logging, mining and

development must be stopped or the planet is doomed.
They hope that by destroying property they can inflict
enough financial damage on companies and individuals to
make them stop their environmentally harmful practices."

Whether we agree or disagree with the ELF mission and/
or tactics, at least ABCNews.com offered a more rounded
description of the leaderless group. In an informed society,
this is precisely how citizens can form educated opinions.

Hammer Time

The Simon and Garfunkel song goes: "I'd rather be a hammer than a nail"

Okay, I'll buy that...but do you know who has it even worse than the nail?

The wood.

I'd rather be the nail than the wood...

Running with the bulls

I remember reading something William Burroughs said about how we humans, like the bull in a bullfight, tend to focus on the elusive red cape instead of the matador. Indeed, we are all-too-easily distracted from the real targets by an attractive image or illusion.

As you know, there *are* some bulls that see right through the red cape, uh, *bullshit*...and quite justifiably introduce the matador to the business end of their horns. But before you mistake that for a lesson and/or inspiration, don't forget that such bulls are promptly killed while the matador is mourned as a brave hero.

So, here's my question: If *every* bull in *every* bullfight were to gore *every* matador, how long would it be before bullfights were a thing of the past?

Top Ten Reasons Why Activists Shouldn't Be "Too Radical"

1. We must be careful not to offend the Average American (AvAm)

2. Self-righteousness is such a turn-off

3. We can't give ammunition to the right wing

4. The AvAm is doing the best he/she can and we shouldn't expect more

5. We can't blame the AvAm because she/he just doesn't know better

6. The AvAm will learn at his/her own pace

7. It's not our place to judge

8. Besides, it's not the AvAm's fault; the Republicans are to blame

9. The AvAm may be indifferent (at best) to reality...but they are still "the people"

10. Why bother? It'll just increase the chances of being arrested and it's way too late anyway

Revolution
just ain't what it used to be

If you were to publicly declare your discontent with the
U.S. government and your subsequent desire to abolish
that government, the land of the free would likely reward
you with an orange jumpsuit and a one-way ticket for an
all-inclusive vacation at Guantanamo Bay.

Now imagine if you instead chose to stand in front of a
crowded room and utter something along these lines:

> I think all men—and women—are created equal and are
> endowed with certain undeniable rights, including life,
> liberty, and the pursuit of happiness. To secure these rights,
> governments are created and derive their powers from the
> consent of the governed. Whenever any form of
> government tries to destroy or take away these undeniable
> rights, it is the right of the people to alter or abolish that
> government and replace it with a new one.

Bingo: you're a high school history teacher. Okay class; turn to page 257. Today we'll be talking about Patrick Henry (and don't tell me "give me liberty or give me death" sounds an awful lot like what an insurgent might say).

Thomas Jefferson can pronounce: "Every generation needs a new revolution." But that doesn't mean I can. Honest Abe once declared: "Any people anywhere being inclined and having the power have the right to rise up and shake off the existing government, and force a new one that suits them better." Hey, I'd love a government that suits me—and most humans—better, but making plans to "shake off the existing government and force a new one" would just about guarantee you a place on that secret no-fly list.

Let's face it, revolution just ain't what it used to be. Mao Tse-Tung warned: "A revolution is not a dinner party, or writing an essay, or painting a picture, or doing embroidery." Today, revolution is a Chevy commercial or a Beatles song. Che Guevara believed "the true revolutionary is guided by great feelings of love." By 1994, Newt Gingrich and his merry band of Republicans were using "revolution" to describe a minor reshuffling of ruling class allegiances. "The most heroic word in all languages is revolution," stated Eugene Debs, but if he were around today and typed "revolution" into Google, he'd find the top response was for a software company.

As long as you're not talking about the U.S. government, you can have as many revolutions as you please. You can have 33 per minute, for all Dick Cheney cares. Fitness, music, film, art, and countless ways to make money—the mutinous mood is alive and well. This time around, however, the revolution was indeed televised and is now enjoying a long, successful run in syndication.

Can the huddled befuddled masses to snap from their self-induced trance to recapture the subversive spirit of '76? I'll give the last word to Abraham Lincoln:

> This country, with its institutions, belongs to the people who inhabit it. Whenever they shall grow weary of the existing government, they can exercise their constitutional right of amending it, or their revolutionary right to dismember or overthrow it.

Remember: Abe said it, not me.

Note to FBI agents and other assorted law enforcement types

If you've made it this far without skimming or spacing out, I congratulate you. I promise the next few sections will really keep your attention.

Who killed Michael Moore?
(Why and what's the reason for?)

There's no shortage of outrage on the Left. Plenty of marches and manifestos to go along with the myriad calls to change this and take back that. Toss in the occasional fighting words and the intermittent flirtation with property damage and the Left typically does just enough to get itself effectively demonized by the mainstream... thus making it that much easier for the police to get away with swinging their nightsticks at the next "anti-globali-zation" protest.

So, here's my question: What would those who identify as leftists do if one of their high profile icons were openly eliminated? For the sake of argument, let's say the U.S. government (or one of its proxies)—with the full support of the corporate media—overtly did away with Michael Moore for his political beliefs and anti-corporate activism.

(Let me clarify something before you send off all those e-mails telling me Moore is a poser, fake, Democrat, opportunist, egomaniac, gatekeeper, whatever. I'm neither endorsing nor condemning Moore here; I'm simply recognizing his current status. In a society as heavily conditioned as ours—a society that defines the "left" to include both Hillary Clinton and Ward Churchill—Michael Moore might as well be Che fuckin' Guevara. In other words, choosing the nation's best-known "rebel" as a target would be nothing less than the government declaring war on dissidents of all stripes.)

So, what would the American left wing do if Moore were deported like Emma Goldman, Charlie Chaplin, and (almost) John Lennon? What if he was railroaded, denied a fair trial, and imprisoned like, say, Mumia Abu-Jamal or Leonard Peltier? What if he was to be publicly executed even in the face of massive protests, e.g. Sacco and Vanzetti, Julius and Ethel Rosenberg, Tookie Williams, or Ken Saro Wiwa of Nigeria? How about an assassi-nation; a straight-out hit job along the lines of Fred Hampton, Malcolm X, Martin Luther King, or even Patrice Lumumba and Salvador Allende?

Pick your poison; it doesn't matter how he's removed. The question remains: What if the U.S. government (or one of its proxies)—with the full support of the corpo-rate media—transparently eliminated Michael Moore for his political beliefs and activism? Would we see anything more than a flood of articles, blog posts, t-shirts, and open letters from Sean Penn? Would the reaction go beyond asking the state for permission to protest and agreeing beforehand how many of those protestors will consent to be arrested? Would Bob Dylan re-write "Who Killed Davey Moore?" and have Bono sing it outside the Pentagon?

If that's the case, perhaps emboldened by the ease with which Moore's eradication was achieved, the government might then toss Noam Chomsky, Derrick Jensen, and Cynthia McKinney into prison for treason. More pro-tests, more outrage, more fundraisers. Undaunted, Cor-porate America pulls all advertising dollars from Jon Stewart and Stephen Colbert and forces their shows off the air. In response, 500 new blogs emerge and the "Free Jon Stewart" website registers nearly a million hits a day until it is hacked and removed.

Shortly thereafter, the government might start spying on American citizens and detaining prisoners without pressing charges while corporations ravage the earth in pursuit of profit, wiping out entire eco-systems in the process. Oops...sorry; they already did all that without being stopped.

Marveling at the relative lack of resistance, the powers-that-be initiate mass arrests of suspected domestic eco-terrorists, culminating in the bombing of several ELF and/or ALF safe houses, leaving dozens dead? (Not possible, you say? Ask the folks at MOVE.) We know what the general public would say...the same thing they say every time a new "security precaution" is instituted: "If it makes us safer, I'm all for it." But how do you think lefty activists and thinkers would react? Could they—would they —do anything to stop the onslaught?

This is not a facetious question, an accusation, or an ill-advised attempt at satire. I'm genuinely curious: What do you think radicals, progressives, liberals, anarchists, socialists, communists, and all such fellow travelers would do if the U.S. government (or one of its pro-xies)—with the full support of the corporate media—blatantly killed Michael Moore for his political beliefs and activism?

Kurt Vonnegut sez: "There is no reason good can't triumph over evil, if only angels will get organized along the lines of the mafia."

America's top exports:
Grief, sorrow, and loss

"Their lives are bigger than any big idea."
—"Peace on Earth," U2

My mother passed away on January 12, 2008…after a long illness. She was nearly 72 and had been very ill since mid-2005. Intellectually, one might think that perhaps I had time to "come to terms" with a sense of inevitably… yet I remain inconsolable. Despite having almost three years to "prepare" for this reality, her death is teaching me previously unimaginable lessons about grief, sorrow, and loss. My heart is broken, shattered in a million pieces.

Amidst my mourning, I can't help but visualize the feelings of grief, sorrow, and loss being experienced in places directly and indirectly impacted by US policies. Imagine if you will, a mother in Iraq. She walks to the market as an American bomb levels her home. Her parents, her husband, her children (none of whom were affiliated with the "insurgency"): all killed. What of *her* grief, sorrow, and loss…as the US continues to spend one million dollars per minute on war?

And it's not just military murders. Every two seconds, somewhere on the planet, a child starves to death. More grief, sorrow, and loss. More anger and frustration, too. Columnist and author Norman Solomon recently shared similar emotions when his mother died. "Our own mourning should help us understand and strive to prevent the unspeakable pain of others," he wrote. "And whatever love we have for one person, we should try to apply to the world."

There's a line in the song, "Middle of the Road" by the Pretenders: "When you own a big chunk of the bloody Third World…the babies just come with the scenery."

What's that…we don't own anything here or in the Third World? Here's the equation, friends: American tax dollars (and our rhetoric and/or our support and/or our silence) fund and/or enable US domination of institutions like the World Bank. As a result, the developing world spends $13 on debt repayment for every $1 it receives in aid. That means untold billions are allocated toward paying off debt to powerful Western banks instead of being invested in water systems, infra-structure to rural communities, education, and health care.

A 2004 UNICEF report on the State of the World's Children found:

- One in six of the children on the planet were severely hungry
- One in seven had no access to health care
- One in five had no safe water
- One in three had no toilet or sanitation facilities at home
- 640 million children did not have adequate shelter
- 140 million children, the majority of them girls, had never been to school

More than 10 million child deaths were recorded in 2003, with an estimated 29,158 children under 5 dying from mostly preventable causes every day.

29,158. Under 5. Every day. From preventable causes.

The next time you're at a baseball game or rock concert, glance around and get a feel for what 29,158 looks like. Then try your best to conceive of the feelings of grief, sorrow, and loss inspired by those 29,158...each and every day. These are humans, not statistics. They feel as much as you or I. If they feel anything like I do right now, they are utterly despondent.

"In mediaspeak and political discourse, the human toll of corporate domination and the warfare state is routinely abstract," wrote Solomon. "But the results—in true human terms—add rage and more grief on top of grief."

These doomed humans cry, they mourn, they miss loved ones, and they ask *why* when the UN tells them that the basic nutrition and health needs of the world's poorest people would cost only $13 billion a year (that's less than 10% of what the US has spent on the war in Iraq so far).

Remember: every two seconds, somewhere on the planet, a child starves to death. Meanwhile, the US spends one million dollars per minute on war. Do the math: How much of our money was spent on war and how many children starved to death while your read this article?

We often hear the question: "Why do they hate us?"

We give them an excellent reason every 2 seconds and a million more reasons every single minute.

Wish you were here

- Long-tailed Hopping-mouse
- Nelson's Rice Rat
- Chadwick Beach Cotton Mouse
- Pemberton's Deer Mouse
- Cape Warthog
- Scioto Pigtoe (clam)
- Barbados Raccoon
- Tahitian Sandpiper
- Okinawa Flying-fox
- Slender-billed Grackle
- Dodo
- Lesser Koa Finch
- Greater Koa Finch
- Mauritian Owl
- White-faced Owl
- Arizona Cotton Rat
- Blue Pike
- Kansas Bog Lemming
- Mexican Grizzly Bear
- Japanese Sea lion

Undoing the Latches:
Recognizing the Gates Around Us

In his brilliant book, *The Pig Who Sang to the Moon: The Emotional World of Farm Animals*, Jeffrey Moussaieff Masson writes:

> I was told by some New Zealand sheep farmers that sometimes a particularly smart lamb will learn to undo the latch of a gate, evidently not an uncommon skill, and the sheep farmer then worries that the lamb might teach his less clever companions to do the same.

Masson asked a group of farmers, "What do you with sheep who can undo the latch?"

"We shoot them," came the reply, "so they can't pass on their knowledge."

"Others nodded in agreement," Masson continued. "They all had anecdotes about particularly intelligent sheep who were shot as a reward for their cleverness."

While this excerpt stands alone as a telling indictment of human behavior in general and the treatment of animals in particular, it additionally reminds one how important it is for each of us to not only undo the latches on the gates that keep our minds imprisoned…but to also pass on that knowledge.

Of course, those who have learned to undo the latches in human society are "rewarded for their cleverness," too. Deported (Emma Goldman), murdered Gestapo-style (Fred Hampton), framed and imprisoned (Leonard Peltier) …the tactics vary, but in America, the tactics are typically more subtle than overt terror.

"It can happen [in the U.S.], but it's not on the scale of a state that really terrorizes its own citizens," says Noam Chomsky.

> If you come from the more privileged classes, if you're a white middle-class person, then the chances that you are going to be subjected to literal state terror are very slight. It

could happen, but it's slight. What will happen is that you'll be marginalized, excluded. Instead of becoming part of the privileged elite, you'll be driving a taxi cab. It's not torture, but very few people are going to select that option, if they have a choice. And the ones who do select it will never be heard from again. Therefore they are not part of the indoctrination system. They don't make it. It could be worse, but it's enough to discipline people.

To a point, it's certainly more than enough to discipline people…but even the most conditioned of societies can be pushed too far and that's when the latches get undone, the knowledge passed on, and the gates fly open.

These gates (usually unrecognized) can lock us into a limited way of seeing things…a concept Masson also touches on in *The Pig Who Sang to the Moon*. He spoke with some women who worked with cattle…asking them about the cows' feelings. "They don't have any," the women agreed. "They are always the same, they feel nothing."

"At that moment," Masson writes, "we all heard a loud bellowing. I asked why the cows were making that noise."

The women shrugged it off as "nothing," explaining that cows that were separated from their calves were calling them. "The calves are afraid," one woman said, "and are calling for their mothers, and their mothers are afraid for their calves and are calling them, trying to reassure them."

"It sounded to me," Masson stated, "as if these people were suffering from... confirmation bias, which involves only taking into account evidence that confirms a belief already held and ignoring or dismissing evidence that disproves that same belief."

Think about that. Even the evidence of their own senses cannot convince them.

There's an important lesson lurking in there for us all: The gatekeepers—often using confirmation bias as their key—are not limited to the elite players in the corporate/government nexus.

Pass it on...

Juxtaposition

There are nearly 2000 diet books currently available at the click of a mouse.

Every two seconds, somewhere on planet earth, a human starves to death.

How many have we lost while you read this book?
(Humans, not diet books)

Tyler Durden sez: "You are not a beautiful and unique snowflake. You are the same decaying organic matter as everyone else, and we are all part of the same compost pile."

(From *Fight Club*, by Chuck Palahniuk)

What I Believe

I believe it would not only be accurate, but also extremely relevant to start referring to the white supremacist, capitalist patriarchy known as "the United States of America" as "the occupied territories."

I believe someone needs to write a definitive book on the Tupamaros of Uruguay.

I believe the sellout of Dennis Kucinich in 2004 should serve as a permanent reminder of what it means to be "progressive" and a Democrat.

I believe it's useful to remember quotes like this one from Malcolm Forbes: "Elected leaders who forget how they got there won't the next time."

I believe that landlords should lower rents once they have paid off their mortgage.

I believe all forms of authority must be questioned...
over and over again.

I believe there is much to learn from the examples of the
Black Panthers, Puerto Rican Young Lords, and Amer-ican
Indian Movement.

I believe the "land of the free" cannot incarcerate its
citizens at the rate of 1200 per week.

I believe the home of the brave cannot carpet bomb
civilians from 15,000 feet and call it "humanitarianism."

I believe that yes, the ruling elite truly can make this
country "what it once was," e.g. an arctic region covered
with ice.

I believe all this talk about "preserving our way of life"
gets to the heart of the matter. "Our" way of life is
precisely the issue.

I believe the current patterns of dissent in America are
long overdue for re-evaluation and overhaul. The powers-
that-be have long ago figured out how to either

marginalize or co-opt dissent. Unless our tactics evolve, they will become self-parody.

I believe Americans seeking change must help cultivate new, more realistic American Dreams (plural)...dreams not for sale to the highest bidder...dreams not based on material consumption or physical beauty. We need dreams that promote and extol unity and collective success while maintaining our individuality and independence...dreams that challenge humans to think for themselves *and* about others.

I believe that too many people imply that unless a critic expounds a specific strategy for change, the critique is worthless or too negative. The problem with this understandable retort is that it misses the crucial role critical analysis plays in a society where problems are so cleverly disguised. When discussing the future, the first step is often an identification and demystification of the past and present. In order to inspire and motivate humans to work for change and try new approaches, we must agree that we got it wrong the first time.

What do *you* believe?

Top Ten Reasons Why the White Supremacist Capitalist Patriarchal Culture (WSCPC) Will Not be Toppled Any Time Soon

1. The "average American" (AvAm) believes in the two-party/land of opportunity/god's country scam
2. The AvAm is too busy "just getting by" to worry about the WSCPC
3. Not tonight, "American Idol" is on
4. Now is not the time; we've got evil-doers to kill, goddammit
5. What passes for dissent usually involves asking permission to hold a sign in a predetermined "free speech zone" for a few hours on a Saturday afternoon
6. To seriously challenge the WSCPC is to invite potential imprisonment and/or physical threat
7. The AvAm would gleefully turn in anyone willing to take such drastic measures to provoke change

8. Decades of intense conditioning have made the WSCPC virtually invisible to the AvAm

9. Uh...what was I saying?

10. Never mind...

Simple Steps Towards Change

Whenever I write an article or give a talk about the state of global affairs, the first question asked is this: "So, what can/should we do?" My inevitably stammering reply involves a combination of three factors:

What we've been doing all along is obviously not working

We need new ideas, new tactics, and a far greater commitment from everyone

I can't say more because it could be (purposely) misconstrued and that just don't fly in the land of the free (*sic*).

Sometimes, when I'm feeling particularly frisky, I might quote Walt Whitman:

This is what you shall do: Love the earth and sun and the animals, despise riches, give alms to everyone that asks, stand up for the stupid and crazy, devote your income and labor to others, hate tyrants, argue not concerning God, have patience and indulgence toward the people, take off your hat to nothing known or unknown, or to any man or number of men—go freely with powerful uneducated persons, and with the young, and with the mothers or families—re-examine all you have been told in school or church or in any book, and dismiss whatever insults your own soul; and your very flesh shall be a great poem.

In an attempt to finally segue from the nebulous to the somewhat tangible, I offer these eight simple Whitman-esque ways everyday Americans can begin to challenge the dominant culture without getting themselves fitted for an orange jumpsuit.

Embrace not the corporate sanctioned standard American diet; go vegan, organic, and local.

Be warned: what you own ends up owning you; say no to conspicuous consumption.

Opt for two wheels, not four; bid a fond farewell to your internal combustion engine.

Under no circumstances should you cast a vote for either a Democrat or a Republican; these are but two wings on one corporate party.

Never, ever, ever trust a liberal (on *anything*).

Reject both war *and* its warriors; offer not your support
to those who volunteer to wage war.

Reach out for your television remote and boldly press
"off" (toss the cell phone, too).

6.6 billion miracles are more than enough; cease
breeding immediately.

(If even 25% of America made these basic, entirely doable
cultural adjustments, it would essentially qualify as a
revolution...by today's diluted standards.)

Mickey Z. sez: "All roads lead to nowhere, but they are always filled."

Wish you were here

West African Black Rhino
declared extinct in July 2006

inspired by Michael Greenwell

An inhuman future

A drone-like female voice booms over the subway
loudspeaker:

> Ladies and Gentlemen, pan-handling is against the law.
> Please do not give to law-breakers. Please give instead to
> charities that support those in need. Thank you.

Let's rewind back to, say, 1973. If some futuristic flick
injected that exact pre-recorded spiel into a futuristic
subway scene, we all would have chuckled at the
representation of such an inhuman future.

Before it's beaten out of us

Back before it was common to see women and girls playing basketball, I remember seeing two black girls, maybe 13 years old bouncing a basketball while waiting for a train at Lexington Avenue.

They were quite good and were obviously enjoying themselves.

Within a few minutes, a white cop came along and admonished them to stop throwing the ball around. The girls frowned and watched him walk away like John Wayne.

One of the girls took the ball and gave it one more toss against the wall.

I may be right or wrong about this but that spirit: making that one last toss against the wall to challenge authority is humanity at its best…

Derrick Jensen sez: "One of the good things about everything being so fucked up—about the culture being so ubiquitously destructive—is that no matter where you look—no matter what your gifts, no matter where your heart lies—there's good and desperately important work to be done."

EXIT POLL

If your life were to be presented on stage, which would it
be?

- ☐   comedy
- ☐   tragedy
- ☐   farce
- ☐   mystery
- ☐   musical
- ☐   all of the above

What would the audience do?

- ☐   laugh
- ☐   cry
- ☐   fall asleep
- ☐   walk out
- ☐   demand a refund
- ☐   all of the above

i have seen the best

minds of my *generation*

destroyed by blindness

About the author

The regular visitors to Mickey Z.'s website have ordained themselves "The Expendables." Mickey asked them to write a collective bio and here's the result:

> Mickey Z.'s voice is the roundhouse kick of activist
> literature...profoundly mistrustful of government in all its
> dreadful guises, while courageously supporting all of us who
> stand against it. Determined to live the words, rather than
> simply to speak them, Mickey Z. doesn't get more readers,
> he just makes more friends. His blog is like a front stoop
> where we all gather to talk over the news, what's happening
> with each other, and generally enjoy each other's company.
> The gentle concern for his fellow humans and the behind-
> the-scenes acts of kindness are surpassed only by the
> cuteness of his dimples.

He can be found on the Web at: www.mickeyz.net

Photo by Sacha Lecca

About the cover

The cover was created by Chuck Gregory from a photo by Michele Zezima. The idea developed from a good bit of discussion between Mickey and Chuck.

About the Publisher

CWG Press is owned and operated by Chuck Gregory in Fort Lauderdale, FL. Rather than limiting our books to a specific genre, we look for books that are of good quality. We choose our authors and our books carefully, and we are proud of them.

 **a small publisher with big ideas**

ISBN 978-0-9788186-2-3

CPSIA information can be obtained at www.ICGtesting.com
Printed in the USA
LVOW11s1324140316

479082LV00001B/47/P